PICTURING SCOTLAND

SCOTLAND'S
MOUNTAINS

NESS PUBLISHING

2 The Cairngorms in their winter majesty, viewed from the north with the Larig Ghru, which cuts right through the Cairngorms, just left of centre.

SCOTLAND'S MOUNTAINS

Welcome to the top of the world!

That's certainly how it feels when your climb is rewarded by endless mountain vistas viewed from your own personal rock, or snowfields stretching away to the next summit. It's the peak-top panoramas which demonstrate better than anything else that Scotland is a land of mountains, more than 500 of which rise to over 2500ft (762m). And that's just the figure for those that rank officially as Munros (3000ft (914m) and over) or Corbetts (2500-2999 ft). If all the subsidiary tops that cluster around the principal summits were added, the number would increase greatly.

But Scotland's mountains should not be judged purely on their height. If assessed on the basis of curious shapes or (in some cases) difficulty of climb, many of the smaller peaks outrank their loftier cousins. Ben Nevis may be the highest – and impressive with it – but when it comes to extraordinary profiles and awesome overhangs, it does not compare with the likes of, for example, Suilven, Stac Pollaidh or The Cobbler (opposite). So it is perfectly possible to get up close and personal with plenty of dramatic mountain 'architecture' without having to trek to the highest tops. A worthwhile climb might only take an hour or two, not all day. To cite another example, the bonnie little peak of Ben A'an pictured on p.1 is a short and not too demanding walk which gives superb views over Loch Katrine in The Trossachs.

Ben Arthur, 884m/2900ft, usually known as The Cobbler, is the most distinctive mountain in the Arrochar Alps and stands above the village of Arrochar.

Given the abundance of books on this subject, it might be fair to wonder what a little tome like this can usefully add to the mix. The answer lies in the vastness of the subject matter: amongst Scotland's mountains there are always new angles to find, different perspectives to picture, alternative compositions to capture. The moods of the mountains are constantly changing with the weather and the seasons (and sometimes you get all weather and all seasons in one day!) so every exploration of the highland wilderness can present a unique experience. This book aims to show something of the varying characteristics of mountain ranges in different parts of the country, some of which are really marked. For example, once you have been to both, you will never mistake the Cairngorms for the Torridons. And the mountains hold their secrets, perhaps none more than the Cairngorms. Those big rounded hills look imposing rather than spectacular as seen from, say, Kingussie or Aviemore; however, venture through the Larig Ghru or up the surrounding summits and a totally different landscape surrounds you. Some of the following pages will illustrate this.

6   The summit of Beinn an Lochain (901m/2956ft) in the Arrochar Alps, from Inveraray, Argyll.

This book takes a journey from south to north, beginning with the Arrochar Alps in the Cowal Peninsula of eastern Argyll. From there a zigzag course takes in west Stirlingshire, Perthshire, Lochaber, the Cairngorms and on via Inverness-shire to Wester Ross for the Torridons and beyond, finishing up in Inverpolly on the fringes of Sutherland. After that we visit the more mountainous of the western islands, from Jura to the Outer Hebrides. The Isle of Mull's Munro, Ben More, is shown opposite and Rum and Eigg are on the back cover.

The fact that Scotland's mountains aren't huge in world terms takes nothing away from the fantastic images they offer or the degree of challenge that climbing many of them presents. After all, the Cuillins of Skye draw climbers from all over the world. Discovering Scotland's mountains can provide a lifetime of adventure, recreation and escape from the daily grind – not to mention plenty of good old-fashioned exercise! Come and see…

Ben More is the highest point on the Isle of Mull at 966m/3169ft.

8   At 1126m/3694ft Ben Cruachan is the highest mountain in Argyll – and a tough climb. Seen here
from many miles to the south, we'll see it again closer up on p.16. It comprises the two summits

seen on the left of the ridge, while the top at the right-hand end is Stob Diamh, classified as a
separate Munro at 998m/3274ft.

10 Up in the Arrochar Alps, viewed from the snowy folds of Ben Donich are Beinn Narnain (926m/3038ft) with the plateau summit, to the right of which is The Cobbler again.

Expeditions on short winter days provide plenty of low-sun images. This is the top of Ben Donich, 11
847m/2779ft. When in need of solitude, try this.

12 Windblown snow sculptures add an artistic touch to a mountainscape. The bright peak in the distance is Ben Lomond.

Ben Lomond is Scotland's southernmost Munro and stands 974m/3195ft high above Loch Lomond. **13**
This view however is from the east, which gives a better impression of its summit corrie.

14 A matching pair of great mountains: in Stirling District, overlooking Crianlarich, are Stob Binnein, left (1165m/3822ft) and Ben More (1174m/3852ft), seen here from Ben Ledi, near Callander.

A classic Scottish scene, with Kilchurn Castle on the shores of Loch Awe and Ben Lui **15** (1130m/3707ft) towering beyond, still snow-capped in mid May.

16 The eastward view along Ben Cruachan's granite ridge towards Ben Diamh. The normal walker's route is a circular one that takes in both summits.

Glen Etive lies north of Ben Cruachan and is lined with mountains, of which Ben Starav (1078m/3537ft) has a particularly imposing presence.

18 Moving to the east and looking into Perthshire from Glen Ogle reveals mighty Ben Vorlich (985m/3232ft), still wearing its winter clothes in mid April.

Engaging with mountains benefits from an ability to embrace conditions which might obscure, but add **19** dramatic lighting to the view. Thus we see Ben Lawers, just in Scotland's top 10 at 1214m/3983ft.

20 Glen Lyon is famed as a wild and beautiful part of Perthshire, captured here in virtual white-out conditions. Up in the snows beyond these foothills is Carn Mairg (1041m/3415ft).

A few miles to the north-east of Carn Mairg is Schiehallion (1083m/3553ft), a mountain with a lot of mystique attached to it, perhaps because its name translates as 'Fairy hill of the Caledonians'.

22 The setting of the Perthshire town of Pitlochry is much enhanced by its position under the steep slopes of Ben Vrackie, a Corbett at 840m/2755ft.

Stately Blair Castle is backed by a group of three Munros known collectively as Beinn a' Ghlo. **23**
One of the three mountains, Carn Liath (975m/3199ft), is seen to the right.

24 Now we head west to Glencoe, Lochaber. Dawn on a winter's day lights up Buachaille Etive Mor, gatekeeper of the south-eastern approach to the glen and one of the most iconic mountains in

Scotland. While it is not particularly high at 1021m/3350ft, it is a challenge for hill-walkers and rock- **25**
climbers alike. Its perfect shape from this side adds to its appeal.

26 Glen Coe is a 'target-rich' environment for mountain-lovers. Here, the famed Aonach Eagach (meaning 'notched ridge') rises above the River Coe. The top of the ridge can be seen in the foreground opposite.

Climbing Bidean Nam Bian (1150m/3773ft) on the south side of Glencoe rewards with this **27** northerly view across Aonach Eagach and the Mamore range, with Ben Nevis in the far distance.

28 At the western end of Glencoe, above the village of South Ballachulish, stands Beinn a' Bheithir. It consists of two Munros, Sgorr Dhearg at 1024m/3360ft (left) and Sgorr Dhonuill, 1001m/3284ft.

If you turn your gaze to the right of the previous view and look out across Loch Leven, **29** you'll be greeted by the sight of Garbh Bheinn (885m/2903ft) across the loch in Ardgour.

30 Further west, in the district of Sunart, Ben Resipol (846m/2766ft) is the highest point west of Ardgour. It is seen here from near Salen in Ardnamurchan.

Returning to Ardgour, a north-westerly view takes in the Mamores, first seen on p.27, with **31** Sgurr a' Mhaim (1099m/3606ft) in the centre clad with a scree slope of whitish crystalline rock.

32 This classic view of Glenfinnan proves that the mountains don't have to be especially high to help create a perfect highland scene. Two Corbetts are located on the southern (left) side of the loch.

Naturally, Ben Nevis (1344m/4406ft) is much photographed, so finding an unusual view is more
challenging. This picture, taken from Glenfinnan about 15 miles away, shows its dominance of the area.

34 The Nevis Range incorporates three more 4000ft mountains, two of which are Aonach Beag (1234m/4049ft) on the left, while Aonach Mor (1221m/4006ft) is the larger mass on the right.

Spectacular lighting is a great but unpredictable gift. Dawn on Loch Lochy and Meall nan Dearcag in **35** the Great Glen are blessed with a fleeting moment of surreal glow.

36 On the eastern edge of Lochaber by Loch Laggan is a group of mountains centred on Creag Meagaidh (1128m/3701ft), left, and Stob Poite Coire Ardair (1054m/3458ft), corniced, on the right

Left: the path from Creag Meagaidh to Stob Poite Coire Ardair traverses this tricky col known as **37** 'The Window'. Right: the corrie lochan under the crags of Creag Meagaidh.

38 Looking into Lochaber from the east across Loch Laggan, Stob Coire Claurigh rises impressively to 1177m/3862ft. It is the easternmost peak in the Ben Nevis/Grey Corries range.

Offering a radical contrast in lighting conditions, another view down Loch Laggan reflects the **39** surrounding hills and mountains.

40 To conclude the Lochaber section of our journey, this view takes in the western end of Glencoe from Ballachulish Bridge. The Pap of Glencoe is on the left with the end of Aonach Eagach to its right.

On the right-hand side of the picture Stob Coire nan Lochan and Bidean Nam Bian are still snow capped in mid April.

42 And so to the Cairngorms. Cairn Gorm itself (1244m/4081ft) rises above Loch Morlich, with the funicular railway visible near the centre of the picture.

Braeriach (1296m/4252ft) shows off its huge corrie, with sheer drops that pose a **43** danger to walkers in bad visibility.

44 This grand vista from Braeriach looks across the Larig Ghru to Ben Macdui, at 1309m/4295ft the second-highest mountain in Scotland. Carn a' Mhaim (1037m/3402ft) is at the end of the ridge.

From the Black Pinnacle near Braeriach's summit, the Cairngorms show a far more rugged aspect **45** than is apparent from a distance. Cairn Toul (1291m/4236ft) towers above Lochan Uaine.

46 Over in the eastern Cairngorms, Lochnagar at 1155m/3789ft stands above the corrie lochan from which it takes its name. Cac Carn Beag, the little tor that forms the summit, can just be seen.

From the corrie rim seen opposite, this is the view down into Lochnagar. The jumble of boulders **47** overhanging the edge does not inspire confidence in their ability to hang on much longer!

48 Moving west once again, this is the famously beautiful Glen Affric in Inverness-shire. Mountains all around, with those in the distance so far away that they are climbed from Kintail in Wester Ross.

Glen nam Fiadh, the valley to the north of Glen Affric, presents this parade of peaks. The nearest is **49** Tom a' Choinich (1112m/3648ft) and the furthest is Mam Sodhail at 1181m/3875ft.

50 The next valley to the north is Glen Cannich. In this winter-wonderland scene, the distant peak towards the right of the picture is Beinn Fhionnlaidh (1005m/3297ft), pronounced 'byn yoony'.

The city of Inverness is not known for having a mountain towering over it, yet with a long lens this **51** is the impression given by Sgurr na Lapaich (1150m/3773ft), actually about 35 miles distant.

52 Heading into Wester Ross, the A87 from Loch Cluanie down into Glen Shiel gives access to no fewer than 21 Munros. Seven of these are on the South Glen Shiel Ridge, visible at the top of the picture.

The Saddle (1010m/3314ft), on the south side of Glen Shiel, is generally reckoned to be **53** the finest mountain in the area.

54 A little further west and into Kintail, A' Ghlas-bheinn (918m/3012ft) boasts a particularly impressive summit ridge.

One of Scotland's best-loved mountain views, the Five Sisters of Kintail. **55**
Three of the summits are Munros.

56 Moving north to the Torridons, this is Corrie Mhic Fhearchair on the eastern flank of Beinn Eighe, regarded as one of the most dramatic corries with its triple-buttress head wall.

Beinn Eighe contains two Munros, the higher of which is Ruadh-stac Mor (1010m/3314ft), which is **57** pictured on the front cover. Here we gain an impression of the rugged landscape between the tops.

58 Liathach is perhaps Torridon's most formidable and massive mountain. Its five-mile ridge has eight separate tops, two of which are classified as Munros. The summit height is 1055m/3461ft.

Next to Liathach is Beinn Alligin (986m/3235ft), which means 'the jewelled hill'. It's certainly a gem **59** in terms of shapeliness and dramatic features, such as the Horns of Alligin at the central top.

60 The forbidding profile of Slioch (981m/3218ft), which stands on the eastern side of Loch Maree, is softened by a touch of Alpenglow as the winter sun goes down.

Towards the northern end of Loch Maree, the combination of loch, rock and mountain creates a **61**
perfect highland picture. The mountain is Beinn Airidh Charr, 791m/2595ft.

62 From the head of Loch Maree and looking east through a gap in the nearer hills, we gain a glimpse of the remote and inaccessible Fisherfield Hills.

When it comes to improbable, gravity-defying cliffs combined with majestic proportions and sheer **63** presence, An Teallach is hard to beat. Of its 10 tops, the highest is Sgurr Ghlas Thuill, 1062m/3484ft.

64 East of An Teallach are the Fannaich mountains, seen here rising above Little Loch Broom. The highest peak is Sgurr Mor, 1110m/3642ft.

The wilderness of Inverpolly, north of Ullapool, is viewed here from Gruinard, with the long ridge of **65** Ben Mor Coigach (743m/2437ft) on the right of the picture.

66 Looking its most defiant from the north, Stac Pollaidh (612m/2007ft) is a classic example of how a smaller mountain can make a big impression – an unforgettable sight.

For those who climb Stac Pollaidh, superb vistas like this await them. Cul Mor (849m/2784ft) **67** is in the distance, with Cul Beag away to the right.

68 Just when you think you must have seen all the most strangely shaped hills and mountains, up pops Suilven (731m/2398ft). Its western massif shows an almost surreal symmetry.

Turning our attention now to the island mountains, the Paps of Jura make a magnificent **69** winter scene. This is their southern aspect, photographed from neighbouring Islay.

70 The three paps are Beinn a' Chaolais, Beinn Shiantaidh and Beinn an Oir, the highest at 785m/2575ft. From its summit looking north, the untamed expanse of Jura stretches into the distance.

The Isle of Skye is world famous for its mountains. These are the Red Cuillins, with Beinn Dearg **71** Mhor (731m/2398ft) on the left and twin-topped Glamaig (775m/2542ft) right of centre.

72 Skye's Black Cuillin ridge has to be seen to be believed, especially when dramatically lit. This view looks north with Sgurr Dearg towards the left of the picture – the Inaccessible Pinnacle, catching the

light, can be seen protruding above the summit. In total, the Cuillin Ridge comprises 18 individual 73 tops, 14 of which are over 914m/3000ft, 11 of which are classed as Munros.

74 From an intermediate level east of the main Cuillin ridge, the crazy shape of Am Basteir (934m/3064ft) is on the skyline towards the left. Sgurr nan Ghillean is near the centre.

From the village of Torrin, Skye, we are treated to the classic view of Bla Bheinn (928m/3045ft) with Loch Slapin in the foreground.

76 The final leg of our journey is to the Outer Hebrides. Here on South Uist, with Loch Druidibeg in the foreground, is the mountainous triumvirate of Hecla, Beinn Choradail and Beinn Mhor.

At 620m/2034ft Beinn Mhor is the highest point on South Uist. From near its summit this view 77 looks north to Beinn Choradail in the middle distance and Hecla beyond.

78 Harris is home to the biggest mountains in the Outer Hebrides, the highest of all being Clisham (799m/2620ft) which provides this south-westerly view just as a passing storm blows away.

Clisham's summit ridge has many outcrops of strangely eroded rocks. With this archetypal image of **79** Scotland's mountains, we conclude this journey – but there are plenty more to come …

Published 2011 by Ness Publishing, 47 Academy Street, Elgin, Moray, IV30 1LR
Phone 01343 549663   www.nesspublishing.co.uk

All photographs © Colin Nutt except pp.21 & 68 © Scotavia Images; pp.24/25 © Ian Evans/
Mountain Images; p.67 © Paul Turner; p.69 © Becky Williamson; pp.72/73 © Alan Gordon/Highland Light

Text © Colin Nutt
ISBN 978-1-906549-17-6

Front cover: Beinn Eighe's main summit; p.1: Ben A'an; p.4: the author's son enjoying Beinn Eighe;
this page: summit cairn, Ben Ledi; back cover: the islands of Rum and Eigg

For a list of websites and phone numbers please turn over >

Websites and phone numbers (where available) for principal regions featured in this book in order of appearance:

Argyll: www.argyllonline.co.uk
     www.visitscottishheartlands.com/areas
Loch Lomond & Trossachs National Park: www.lochlomond-trossachs.org (T) 01389 722600
Perthshire: www.perthshire.co.uk (T) 0845 2255 121
Lochaber: www.lochaber.com
Glen Coe: www.glencoe-nts.org.uk (T) 0844 493 2222
Cairngorms National Park Authority: www.cairngorms.co.uk (T) 01479 873535
Tourist Information Centres: www.visithighlands.com
Torridon mountains: www.torridonmountains.com
Isle of Skye: www.isleofskye.com
     www.skyewalks.co.uk
The Cuillins: www.munromagic.com
The Outer Hebrides: www.visithebrides.com/islands
South Uist: www.southuist.com
Harris: www.explore-harris.com